Fly to the Rescue!

retold by Vita Jiménez

illustrated by Kathleen McCord

PAIRED READ Animal Traits 13

Long ago, there was a splendid river. Its water had a very special taste. Every animal liked it.

One day, Moose stopped
at the river for a drink. He
liked the water a lot. So he
drank and drank and drank.

Two beavers were watching.

"Moose is drinking all our water," they said.

Four muskrats were
watching, too.

"We must stop Moose,"
they said.

Eight fish spoke up.

"What about us?" they said.
"We need to live in water."

The fish looked at the beavers and said, "Tell Moose to go away."

The beavers shook their heads. "No way," they said. "Moose is huge!"

Fly heard the animals talking.

"Maybe I can help," said Fly.

The animals smiled. "What help can a little fly give us?"

Fly said, "I will let Moose carry me."

"Then what?" asked the animals.

"You must wait and see," said Fly.

Fly sat on Moose. He waited
and waited. Then he bit
Moose's leg. Moose stomped
his foot. Fly held on. Moose
stomped harder and harder.
The ground sank, and water
rushed in.

Moose ran away.

"The small can win if they use their brains," Fly said.

The animals jumped and clapped.

Respond to Reading

Retell

Use your own words to retell *Fly to the Rescue!* in order.

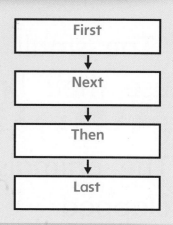

First
↓
Next
↓
Then
↓
Last

Text Evidence

1. Which animals speak first? Sequence

2. What happens after Fly bites Moose? Sequence

3. How do you know that *Fly to the Rescue!* is a folktale? Genre

Compare Texts
Read about the animals in *Fly to the Rescue!*

Animal Traits

What animal flies? What animal swims? Read about different animals in the chart.

Fly	Beaver
Flies have five eyes.	Beavers have strong front teeth.
They have two antennae. The antennae help flies find food.	They use their teeth to chop down trees.
Flies drink their food. They turn food into liquid first.	Beavers build dams and lodges.
Flies can move very fast.	Beavers have webbed back feet that help them swim.

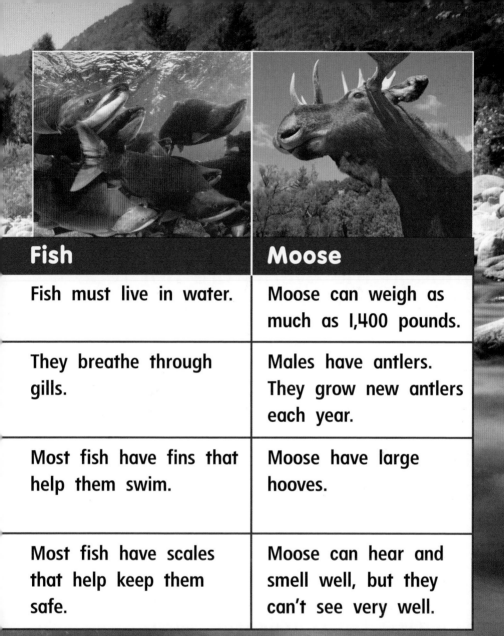

Fish	Moose
Fish must live in water.	Moose can weigh as much as 1,400 pounds.
They breathe through gills.	Males have antlers. They grow new antlers each year.
Most fish have fins that help them swim.	Moose have large hooves.
Most fish have scales that help keep them safe.	Moose can hear and smell well, but they can't see very well.

Make Connections

Look at both selections. What did you learn that you didn't know before? Text to Text

Focus on
Genre

Folktale A folktale is a story based on customs and traditions. Folktales often teach a lesson even though the events are not real.

What to Look for Fly says, "The small can win if they use their brains." Fly is teaching us a lesson. The animals in the story talk. Real animals don't talk.

Your Turn

Make up a folktale with talking animals that teach a lesson. Present your folktale to the class.